DATE DUE		

TERRORISM IN TODAY'S WORLD

Suicide Bombings
In Israel
and Palestinian Terrorism

MICHAEL V. USCHAN

CURRICULUM CONSULTANT: MICHAEL M. YELL
National Board Certified Social Studies Teacher,
Hudson Middle School, Hudson, Wisconsin

WORLD ALMANAC® LIBRARY

Please visit our web site at: www.worldalmanaclibrary.com
For a free color catalog describing World Almanac® Library's list of high-quality books
and multimedia programs, call 1-800-848-2928 (USA) or 1-800-387-3178 (Canada).
World Almanac® Library's fax: (414) 332-3567.

Library of Congress Cataloging-in-Publication Data

Uschan, Michael V., 1948-
    Suicide bombings in Israel and Palestinian terrorism / Michael V. Uschan.
      p. cm. – (Terrorism in today's world)
    Includes bibliographical references and index.
    ISBN 0-8368-6561-8 (lib. bdg.)
    ISBN 0-8368-6568-5 (softcover)
    1. Terrorism–Israel–Juvenile literature   2. Suicide bombings–Israel–Juvenile literature.
    3. Arab-Israeli conflict–1993–Juvenile literature.   I. Title.   II. Series
    HV6433.I75U83   2006
    956.9405'4–dc22   2005043690

This North American edition first published in 2006 by
World Almanac® Library
A Member of the WRC Media Family of Companies
330 West Olive Street, Suite 100
Milwaukee, WI 53212 USA

Managing Editor: Tim Cooke
Designer: Steve Wilson
Picture Researcher: Laila Torsun
World Almanac® Library editor: Alan Wachtel
World Almanac® Library art direction: Tammy West
World Almanac® Library design: Dave Kowalski
World Almanac® Library production: Jessica Morris and Robert Kraus

Picture credits: Front Cover: Empics: Abaca Press BRG: 13; Corbis: Gyori Antoine/Sygma
20, Bettmann 27, Reuters 4/5, 6, 8, 36/37, Peter Turnley 17, Koren Ziv/Sygma 10/11;
Empics: AP 18; Getty Images: Keystone/Stringer/ Hulton 29; Rex Features: Sipa Press 15,
22/23, 31, NN/Keystone USA 32/33, KU/Keystones USA 39, Israel Sun 42; Robert
Hunt Library: 24; Topham Picturepoint: IMW 41; United Nations Photo: Stephenie
Hollyman 35.

Printed in United States of America

1 2 3 4 5 6 7 8 9 10 09 08 07 06

CONTENTS

Cover photo: Army experts examine a bus blown up by a Palestinian suicide bomber in Jerusalem on June 18, 2002. The bomb's eighteen victims included a number of children on their way to school.

CHAPTER ONE

Ayat al-Akhras: A Suicide Bomber

The aim of terrorism is to spread terror. Terrorists seek to achieve their goals by using violence to make large numbers of people afraid enough to give in to their demands. Terrorist groups are usually small, and their actions, such as bombings and kidnappings, often have few victims. Such acts, however, are planned to make whole societies or groups of people afraid of falling victim to similar attacks. Terrorists' aims vary: some believe that they are acting from religious motives, for example, while others want to create an independent state. Some Palestinian suicide bombers want to create a nation on land currently occupied by Israel, while others seek the destruction of Israel itself. Many Muslim Palestinian terrorists also claim to be inspired by their religion, Islam.

▼ Israeli rescue teams clear up some of the damage done to the supermarket by Ayat al-Akhras's suicide bombing.

A Blast in the Supermarket

On the morning of March 29, 2002, Ayat al-Akhras quietly left her parents' home in Dehaishe, a refugee camp for Palestinians in the West Bank near Bethlehem. Later that afternoon, the pretty 18-year-old girl entered the Supersol market in Jerusalem, Israel, which was less than 4 miles (6 km) from where she lived. The store was crowded with people who were buying food they would prepare for the celebration of Passover, an important Jewish holiday.

Ayat, however, was not a shopper. She was a suicide bomber. When Ayat detonated the belt full of explosives she was wearing around her waist, the blast killed her and two other people and wounded more than twenty others.

Bitter Conflict

Palestinian suicide bombers such as Ayat have been terrorizing Israelis since the early 1990s. But the conflict between Palestinian Arabs and Israel dates back at least to the birth of Israel, in 1948. By 1947, the United Nations had drawn up a plan to establish separate Jewish and Arab nations in Palestine, a region where Jews and Arabs had lived together for centuries. The Arabs rejected the plan, but the Jews went ahead with the creation of Israel, a Jewish state, in 1948. Thousands of Arabs left Palestine for other places in the Middle East, with many going to refugee camps. Since then, most Palestinian Arabs have been bitterly opposed to Israel. They also oppose the Israeli occupation of the West Bank and the Gaza Strip, two territories adjacent to Israel proper where most Palestinian Arabs now live. Palestinian Arabs want to create their own state in the region of Palestine. Many Palestinians agree that this state should exist on land that is now part of the Occupied Territories. Some Palestinians, however,

insist that Israel should not exist at all and should be destroyed.

Not all Palestinians, of course, seek Israel's desruction or support violence toward Israelis. Many believe that Palestinians and Israel should negotiate peacefully. But some Palestinian extremists believe that the only way to achieve their goals is through terrorism. With the rise of suicide bombers, the conflict has turned even more deadly. Powerful explosives have made it easy for suicide bombers to kill many people instantly.

The First Suicide Bombers

The news media first used the term *suicide bomber* in 1983, when a Muslim terrorist group called Hezbollah attacked U.S. facilities in Beirut, Lebanon. On October 23, 1983, a member of the group driving a truck full of explosives blew himself up, killing not only himself but 241 U.S. Marines.

This new terrorist tactic was first used by a Palestinian on April 16, 1993. On that day, Sahar Tamam Nabulsi drove a small van loaded with gas canisters into two buses at a restaurant in Israel near Mechola in the Jordan Valley. The resulting explosion killed Nabulsi and another Palestinian and wounded eight Israelis. Since then, an estimated 130 suicide bombing attacks throughout Israel have killed more than 600 people, mainly Israeli Jews, and wounded several thousand more.

▼ At the time Ayat al-Akhras killed herself, she was engaged to be married. Her fiancé said that, if he had known what she was planning to do, he would have stopped her.

A Terrorist Weapon

Suicide bombings aim to terrify ordinary Israelis until they force their government to change its policy toward the Palestinians. They have spread fear throughout Israel, where stores, restaurants, and even buses have armed security guards to try to prevent bombings.

To Palestinian terrorists, suicide bombings are a powerful weapon in their ongoing battle with Israel. Sheikh Ahmed Yassin, an extremist who founded Hamas, a terror group that has staged many suicide bombings, claimed: "The Palestinian people do not have Apache helicopters or F-16s [jet planes] or tanks or missiles. The only thing they can have is themselves, to die as martyrs."

In referring to suicide bombers, Yassin carefully used the term *martyr*. To Muslims, martyrs are people who die while fighting for Islam. The Arab name for a male martyr is *shahid* and for a woman *shahida*. Thus, many suicide bombers do not think of themselves as killers of innocent people but as heroes who sacrifice themselves to spread fear among people they see as enemies of Islam.

Ayat the Bomber

Ayat had a bright future and did not seem to be the kind of person who would want to die for any reason. A good student, she planned to attend Bethlehem University and wanted to become a journalist. She was also going to be married in July 2002.

The question everyone asked after Ayat's death was: "Why did she blow herself up?" Ayat believed that Israel had illegally occupied her people's homeland since 1948 and had treated Palestinians unfairly and brutally during that period. One reason Ayat wanted to become a journalist was to tell the world about the suffering of the Palestinian people.

One report says that the event that made Ayat want to become a suicide bomber occurred when a friend's brother was shot in a raid by Israeli

Martyrs or Murderers?

To Israelis and people in Western countries, suicide bombers are terrorists who murder innocent people and terrify whole communinities. Some opponents of the tactic use the term *homicide bomber* to reflect its murderous intent. Many Palestinians, however, honor suicide bombers as martyrs who sacrifice their lives for Islam by fighting Israel, a Jewish nation. Muslims and Jews had coexisted peacefully for centuries in the Middle East, and they still do in other parts of the world. Since the creation of Israel in 1948,

however, Jews and Muslim Arabs have clashed over control of areas of territory.

Many Muslims, including some Palestinians, argue that suicide bombers should not be praised as martyrs because the Koran, Islam's holy book, condemns killing innocent people as a sin. Critics of the suicide bombings claim that Muslims who support them on religious grounds are using twisted reasoning in backing brutal acts the only purpose of which is to terrorize Israelis.

Female Suicide Bombers

Ayat al-Akhras is part of a new trend in Palestinian terrorism that began in 2002—female suicide bombers. The first was Wafa Idris, a nurse for the Red Crescent (part of the Red Cross). On January 27, 2002, Idris detonated a bomb in Jerusalem. She killed an Israeli man and wounded 150 other people. Many Palestinian women thought that Idris had shown that women could also fight the Israelis. One of them was Fatima Mohammed, a 30-year-old religious studies student. She said: "I was very happy. I thought about how our enemy was shaking with fear and that they were shaking because of a woman." By August 2005, eight Palestinian women had carried out suicide attacks against Israelis. Fifty-nine more women who were sent on suicide missions by terrorist groups were arrested before they could carry out their attacks.

▼ Palestinians celebrate Ayat al-Akhras's bombing outside her family home. Terrorist groups organize celebrations of bombings.

troops. He and other members of the family might have been linked to the Al-Aqsa Martyrs' Brigade, which had conducted many suicide bombings. Another story says that it was the killing by Israeli troops of three of her cousins, who were members of Hamas.

The *Isshtadad*

Ayat contacted Al-Aqsa Martyrs' Brigade and volunteered for an *Isshtadad*, the Arabic word for a suicide bombing. The group helped her plan an attack.

A few days before the bombing, Ayat went to the home of an Al-Aqsa leader to make a videotape that the group would later distribute to TV stations to publicize her act. On it, Ayat criticized Arab men for not having the courage she did to attack Israel: "Shame on the Arab [men] who are sitting and watching the girls of Palestine fighting while they are sleeping."

Ayat left her home on March 29 without telling her parents what she

was going to do. She walked to Jerusalem through fields to avoid the checkpoints on roads where Israeli soldiers watched for suicide bombers. In the city, an accomplice gave her an explosive belt that was loaded with bits of metal which would injure people when the bomb was detonated. He then drove her to the market.

When Ayat tried to enter Supersol at 1:49 P.M., an elderly security guard became suspicious and tried to stop her. Ayat then detonated the bomb, killing herself, the guard, and Rachel Levy, a young Israeli girl.

Joy, Sadness, and Shock

Ayat's parents learned of her death while watching a TV news story about the bombing. A short while later, members of Al-Aqsa Martyrs' Brigade gathered outside the family's home. They fired guns in the air to celebrate Ayat's deed and honor her as a martyr.

Although many Palestinians rejoiced that a blow had been struck against Israel, Ayat's loved ones were deeply saddened. Mohammed al-Akhras, her father, claimed, "Nobody should have to experience this kind of loss. We don't want any more killing."

People around the world were shocked that a young girl had killed herself. They were also saddened that one of her victims was Rachel Levy, a young girl who like Ayat had so much to live for. Their deaths made the incident seem more horrible than other bombings. The two girls appeared together on the cover of *Newsweek* magazine. U.S. president George W. Bush expressed the sorrow that many people around the world felt about the young girls: "When an 18-year-old Palestinian girl is induced to blow herself up, and in the process kills a 17-year-old Israeli girl, the future itself is dying."

Two Daughters, Two Grieving Mothers

One victim of Ayat al-Akhras's suicide attack was Rachel Levy, a seventeen-year-old Israeli girl. Rachel had grown up just a few miles from Ayat, but the two girls had never met. Sealed borders with checkpoints separate Israel from the territories where most Palestinians live, making friendly contact between the two peoples almost impossible. In the eyes of the world, however, the bombing, will forever link Ayat and Rachel together.

The deaths also united their mothers, who grieved for the deaths of both girls. Although Avigail Levy could not understand why Ayat wanted to kill her daughter, she felt sorry for the Arab girl's death: "The other girl was beautiful too, just like my Rachel." And Khadra al-Akhras understood that the pain Rachel's mother felt was as deep as the sorrow she experienced for Ayat: "I loved my daughter the way she loved hers and I suffer for her and for me."

CHAPTER TWO

Palestinian Terrorist Groups

By its very nature, a suicide bombing is an extremely personal act. The bomber is committed to dying along with the victims. But though a single suicide bomber may carry out a devastating attack, suicide bombers rarely work alone. In most cases, suicide bombings are only possible through the efforts of terrorist organizations. Several groups recruit bombers and help them plan and execute their attacks. Palestinian terrorist groups like Hamas, the Al-Aqsa Martyrs' Brigade, and Islamic Jihad are ultimately responsible for most suicide bombings.

"Shaking Off" the Israelis

Suicide bombings may be partly motivated by hatred for Israel, but they are also part of a strategy to achieve specific goals. These goals differ among various terrorist groups. Some extremists want to create a Palestinian state in the West Bank and the Gaza Strip—a goal shared by many moderate Palestinians who do not support terrorism. Other extremists want to destroy Israel and establish an Islamic state in all of Palestine. No matter what their goals, however, the extremists all share a determination to use terror against Israelis. One terrorist, Anwar Aziz, died in December 1993 during a failed attempt to kill Israelis with a stolen ambulance loaded with explosives. Before his mission, he explained why he believed it would

▼ Palestinians throw stones at Israeli troops in Jerusalem during protests in October 2000.

help create an Islamic state: "Battles for Islam are won not through the gun but by striking fear into the enemy's heart."

Most of the current conflict centers on the Israeli presence in the West Bank and the Gaza Strip. Both of these Arab-dominated areas border Israel. The West Bank lies between Israel and Jordan. Its name stems from the fact that the area is located on the west bank of the Jordan River, which makes up part of the Israeli border with Jordan. The Gaza Strip is a small slice of land on the Mediterranean Sea, bordering Israel and Egypt just southwest of Israel proper. In 1967, Israel was left in control of the two areas after it won the Six-Day War against Arab nations. The West Bank and Gaza are widely referred to as "the Occupied Territories" to acknowledge the fact that they are not part of any nation.

In 1987, the anger Palestinians felt over Israel's presence in a land they considered their rightful home erupted into widespread violence against Israeli soldiers and civilians. Called the intifada—an Arabic word that means

"shaking off," referring to getting rid of Israeli control—this violent uprising included terrorist attacks against Israelis in the Gaza Strip, West Bank, and Israel. Other acts of violence included shootings and stabbings of Israel civilians, and artillery attacks from the Occupied Territories and Israel's neighbors on targets inside Israel.

Dashed Hopes for Peace

The intifada ended after Israel and the Palestine Liberation Organization (PLO), which represented the political interests of Arabs in the West Bank and Gaza Strip, signed a peace agreement on September 13, 1993. This pact is known as the Oslo Accords because it was agreed upon in the capital of Norway, Oslo.

By the terms of the Oslo Accords, Israel recognized the PLO, which it had previously declared an illegal organization. In return, PLO chairman Yasser Arafat agreed to end the intifada and to give up the PLO's long-standing claim to land within Israel itself. The Accords set up an interim period during which Israel would withdraw or redeploy its forces in the Occupied Territories and allow the Palestinians a limited amount of self-government.

The Accords were a significant development in the Arab-Israeli conflict. However, they put off some of the most difficult issues, such as the status of East Jerusalem, which both sides claim, and the Israeli settlements built in the Occupied Territories.

Over the next few years, Israel vacated parts of the Occupied Territories and allowed the Palestinians limited self-rule. Violence, however, continued. From 1993 to 2000, about 120 Israelis died in nearly thirty separate terrorist attacks. In 1995, an Israeli extremist assassinated Prime Minister Yitzhak Rabin, who had negotiated the Accords.

In 2000, talks between the two sides about the issues that had been put off in the Oslo Accords broke down. In September that year, Israeli political leader Ariel Sharon visited the Temple Mount in Jerusalem, a site that is sacared to both Jews and Muslims but is under Muslim control. Although Muslim clerics had granted Sharon permission for his visit, it sparked a new upsurge of Palestinian violence that is known as the second intifada. Violence subsided significantly after the death of Yasser Arafat in 2004. Some terrorist groups announced that they would suspend hostilities, but suicide bombings have continued.

> In 2000, talks between the two sides about the key issues that had been put off in the Oslo Accords broke down

Islamists and Nationalists

Palestinian terrorist groups may use the same tactics, but they differ in their goals and in their guiding philosophies.

The Shape of the Region

These maps show different ways the region known as Palestine has been divided. 1. In 1917, the area became a British mandate; in 1923, the British divided the mandate into Transjordan (later Jordan) and Palestine. 2. After the creation of Israel in 1948, the first Arab-Israeli war left Jordan occupying territory earmarked for a Palestinian state on the West Bank, while Egypt occupied the Gaza Strip. 3. After another war in 1967, Israel was left in control of the West Bank and Gaza Strip , as well as the Golan Heights (part of Syria) and the Sinai Peninsula (part of Egypt). Israel later annexed the Golan Heights, but returned Sinai to Egypt. 4. Israel pulled out of the Gaza Strip but remains in control of the West Bank; the Palestinian Authority has varying degrees of power in these territories.

Sacred to Three Religions

The area known as Palestine contains sites that are sacred to three of the world's major religions—Judaism, Islam, and Christianity. It is the biblical Holy Land where Judaism and Christianity were born and where many events important to both religions occurred, including the birth and death of Jesus Christ and many other episodes from the Bible. Muslims consider the region sacred because they believe that the Prophet Muhammad, who founded Islam in A.D. 610 , ascended to heaven from the Temple Mount in Jerusalem.

The importance of the region means that, for much of its history, various rulers have allowed free access to the region's holy sites for followers of all three religions. Muslims and Jews lived peacefully in the region for hundreds of years. At certain times, however, there have been violent clashes over control of the area. The fiercest battles took place from the eleventh to the thirteenth centuries, when Christian armies from Europe launched the wars known as the Crusades in an ultimately unsuccessful attempt to gain control from the region's Muslim rulers.

The groups may be divided into two categories: Islamist and nationalist.

Islamists are Muslims who believe that the rules and practices of Islam, the Muslim religion, should be incorporated into political systems that govern the places where Muslims live. Islamist terrorist groups, such as Hamas and Islamic Jihad, want to establish an Islamic government for all of Palestine, which would include not just the Occupied Territories but Israel, as well. For these groups, achieving their goals would mean the destruction of Israel. They claim that they are fighting a jihad, an Arabic word that some Muslim clerics say means a holy war fought by Muslims against non-believers. In May 2001, Hamas suicide bomber Mahmoud Ahmed Marmash killed five people and wounded 74 in the Israeli city of Netanya. The videotape he recorded before his attack expresses the deadly nature of Islamist philosophy: "God's justice will prevail only in jihad and in blood and in corpses."

Nationalist groups also want to regain complete control of the West Bank and Gaza Strip, but they want to set up civilian governments, not a society based on Islam (some Palestinians are Christians rather than Muslims). Unlike the Islamist groups, which claim all of Israeli territory, some of the nationalist groups have formally acknowledged Israel's right to exist as a separate nation, as the PLO did at Oslo in 1993. The major nationalist Palestinian groups include Tanzim and the Popular Front for the Liberation of Palestine (PFLP).

Despite the differences in their philosophies, Islamist and nationalist groups share many characteristics. They are all committed to forcing Israel to give up at least the Occupied Territories for the creation of a Palestinian state. The groups also believe that they are morally justified in using terrorist tactics to secure that goal.

Palestinian Terrorist Groups

One of the most powerful terrorist organizations is Hamas, whose name is an acronym of the Arabic words

▼ Muslim girls gather at a 2004 rally at the Dome of the Rock Mosque, in Jerusalem, one of the holiest sites in Islam.

Harakat al-Muqawamah al-Islamiyya, which means Islamic Resistance Movement. *Hamas* itself is an Arabic word that means courage or bravery, qualities Hamas expects its members to show in opposing Israel. The organization began as the Palestinian branch of the Muslim Brotherhood, an Egyptian Islamist group that has opposed non-Islamic influence in the Middle East since the 1930s, including the Jewish presence in the region.

Hamas was founded at the start of the first intifada. Its covenant, the document of its principles, claims all of the historic territory of Palestine, including all of Israel. It rejects all diplomacy and says that, "There is no solution to the Palestinian problem

except by Jihad." Hamas was responsible for the first suicide bombing in the conflict. During the second Intifada, Hamas was responsible for nearly half of all suicide bombings, far more than any other single group. The group became popular with some Palestinians for carrying out bombings like one on a summer evening in Tel Aviv in June 2001. A suicide bomber killed 22 Israeli teenagers who were lined up waiting to get into a discotheque.

Hamas has also won the hearts of many people in the West Bank and Gaza Strip by providing the poor with schools, medical clinics, and other social services. Despite its charitable work, Hamas remains committed to terrorism, although it has sometimes suspended terrorist attacks to allow diplomatic moves to take place.

Palestinian Islamic Jihad is a branch of the Egyptian Islamic Jihad. Fathi Shaqaqi started the Palestinian group during the 1970s and led it for two decades. Islamic Jihad was responsible for many suicide bombings during both intifadas from operational bases it established in West Bank Palestinian communities like Hebron and Jenin.

The Al-Aqsa Martyrs' Brigade also began during the second intifada; it was the organization that sent Ayat al-Akhras to blow up the Supersol market in Jerusalem in March 2002. The group is named after al-Aqsa, a historic mosque in Jerusalem. Al-Aqsa Martyrs' Brigade sees itself as a military arm of Fatah, the political party that controls the Palestinian Authority (PA), the Palestinian agency that has some governing powers in areas of the West Bank and Gaza Strip. The word *Fatah*

Sheik Yassin — Founder of Hamas

One of the most mysterious and powerful Palestinian leaders was Sheikh Ahmed Yassin, who founded Hamas and led it for many years despite being paralyzed and nearly blind. Yassin was born in 1937. When Israel was founded in 1948, his family moved to a refugee camp in the Gaza Strip.

Despite being confined to a wheelchair after being paralyzed in a gymnastics accident when he was fourteen, Yassin became a militant dedicated to opposing Israel. Be-

cause Yassin was an Islamic preacher, or *khatib*, some Muslim Palestinians believed him when he said there was nothing wrong with killing innocent people in suicide bombings. Yassin insisted that Hamas was carrying out a legitimate armed campaign. He said: "I reject any classification of us as terrorist." In March 2004, the 67-year-old Yassin was killed when an Israeli helicopter fired a missile at the sheik and his bodyguards as they were leaving a Gaza City mosque. The Israeli action was a response to Hamas violence.

means victory in Arabic; it is also a reverse acronym for Harakat Tahrir el Wataniyeha Filistiniyeh, which means "Palestine Liberation Movement."

Several other Palestinian groups have also commit suicide bombings in Israel. They include Tanzim, which like Al-Aqsa Martyrs' Brigade, is an arm of Fatah; the Popular Front for the Liberation of Palestine; and the Palestine Liberation Front.

Wooing Suicide Bombers

Palestinian terrorist groups are always searching for people who are angry enough to sacrifice their lives to hurt Israel. One way they do this is by attending funerals of Palestinians who have been killed in clashes with Israeli soldiers. At funerals, terrorists seek out mourners who are angry over the death of loved ones, like Ayat al-Akhras. The terrorists try to convince these people to become suicide bombers. They tell them that giving up their lives in a *jihad* will earn them an eternity in paradise (heaven).

If Israel responds to a suicide bombing with violence against the people who organized it, more Palestinians may be killed or injured. That can sometimes create more volunteers to become bombers.

Glorifying the Bombers

Terrorist groups also recruit adults in religion classes. In addition to explaining the Koran and tenets of Islam, extremist religious teachers who support terror organizations try to

▲ Terrorist groups target funerals like that of PLO military leader Abu Jihad, who was killed by Israel commandos, as events to try to recruit new suicide bombers.

make their students angry enough to become bombers by talking about injustices they claim the Israelis have done to Palestinians. They also tell their students about the heavenly glory they could gain if they became a martyr in the long conflict against Israel. Terrorist groups also glorify suicide bombers among the Palestinian public by putting up posters commemorating their deeds, staging rallies in honor of their deaths, and sponsoring television and radio programs about them.

The effort to recruit suicide bombers is even aimed at children. Terrorist groups use many methods to

▲ Hamas suicide bomber Hafez Saleh al-Nazar reads a statement on a video recorded the day before he blew himself up in a car bomb at an Israeli military checkpoint on July 9, 2001. No one else was killed in the attack.

make youngsters think that becoming a bomber is a good thing. In the past even the Palestinian Authority (PA), which governs the Occupied Territories and is supposed to oppose terrorism, has joined this effort. On the "Children's Club," an educational show the PA sponsors for children, a young boy sings a song that includes these lyrics: "When I wander into Jerusalem, I will become a suicide bomber."

Groups like Islamic Jihad have operated summer camps to convince youngsters to become bombers. Said Islamic Jihad member Mohammed el Hattab: "We are teaching the children that suicide bombing is the only thing that makes the Israeli people very frightened [and] that we have the right to do it." Some Palestinian schools teach students that killing Israelis is a noble deed. Palestinian textbooks distort history by claiming that Israelis have no lawful claim to Israel, even though the United Nations authorized the creation of the new nation.

Many people, including some Palestinians, condemn terror groups for trying to persuade children and teenagers to become suicide bombers.

Deadly Suicide Bombings

Since the first Palestinian suicide bombing in 1993, more than 600 Israelis have been killed and thousands injured in more than 130 separate suicide bombings. In some cases, the suicide bombers kill only themselves, but sometimes their attacks claim many victims. Below are some of the bombings in which large numbers of people died:

February 25, 1996—Twenty-six people killed on a bus in Jerusalem.

July 30, 1997—Sixteen people killed in two consecutive bombings in a market in Jerusalem.

June 1, 2000—Twenty-one people killed and 120 wounded outside a discotheque near Tel Aviv's Dolphinarium.

August 9, 2001—Fifteen people killed and about 130 injured at the Sbarro pizzeria in Jerusalem.

March 27, 2002—Thirty people killed and 140 injured in the Park Hotel in Netanya.

January 5, 2003—Twenty-two people killed and about 120 wounded in a double bombing near a Tel-Aviv bus station.

August 19, 2003—Twenty-three people killed and over 130 wounded on a bus in Jerusalem.

October 4, 2003—Twenty-one people killed and 60 wounded in the Maxim restaurant in Haifa.

October 7, 2004—Thirty-two people killed and 120 wounded in bombings at two Sinai holiday resorts in Egypt that are popular with Israelis.

The New-York-based group Human Rights Watch said in 2004 that at least ten suicide bombers who had blown themselves up during the second intifada were under eighteen years of age, including Ayat al-Akhras, who it says was only seventeen at the time of her attack. The group said that, even though all attacks on civilians were illegal, using children to carry them out was particularly wicked.

Critics say that child suicide bombers do not fully understand what they are doing, and they say that children are an easy target for terrorist propaganda. After her sixteen-year-old son blew himself up on a mission for the Popular Front for the Liberation of Palestine, Samir Abdullah said: "It's immoral to send someone so young. They should have sent an adult who understands the meaning of his deeds."

Hussam Abdo was fifteen in 2004 when he was arrested by Israeli troops before he could set off his suicide bomb. In prison afterward, he explained why he had decided to become a bomber: "The reason was because my friend was killed. The second reason I did it is because I didn't want to go to school." Hussam believed that suicide bombers were heroes. He said, "I would become a martyr and go to my God. It's better than being a singer or a footballer. It's better than everything."

Staging a Suicide Bombing

People who want to become suicide bombers sometimes act alone but they more often need the help of terror groups. The attacks can require many people to plan and carry them out.

One of the most terrible bombings was conducted by Hamas on March 27, 2002, when Muhammad Abd al-Basset Oudeh killed thirty people in the Park Hotel in the seafront resort of Netanya. The victims were Israelis celebrating the Passover Seder, an important Jewish celebration.

To carry out the attack, Hamas coordinated the activities of more than a dozen people. Some of the

conspirators made the explosive belt for the bomber, which contained 20 pounds of explosives and metal pieces that flew through the air to wound and kill people. Others prepared false documents so Oudeh could illegally cross the border from the West Bank into Jerusalem. Conspirators also drove Oudeh to the bomb site. To publicize the bombing, one person videotaped Oudeh explaining why he was carrying out the attack and prepared posters of Oudeh holding a rifle in a heroic pose.

The day of the bombing, Oudeh shaved off his beard and mustache and put on a wig so that he would look like a woman. This made him seem less threatening to security guards at the attack site because, at the time, women did not usually conduct attacks. The

▼ Children in a Palestinian school look at young people's drawings of the intifada; some Palestinian schools encourage students to see terrorists as heroes.

explosive belt was concealed beneath his clothes. The disguise enabled Oudeh to walk past guards into a large dining room at the hotel which was filled with over 200 men, women, and children celebrating Passover. He then detonated the bomb.

Terrorist groups can also coordinate simultaneous bombings by two or more bombers. A simultaneous suicide bombing, for example, occurred on August 31, 2004, when two men blew themselves up on buses in Beersheba. The two bombs exploded within seconds of each other.

Yaacov Cohen, who was driving the second bus, said: "I heard a huge blast and saw smoke everywhere. I realized it was an explosion on a bus near me, so I stopped my bus and opened all the doors thinking, 'We should just flee.' Suddenly there was another blast inside my bus. When I opened the doors, a lot of people managed to get out. . . ."

The lethal attack, which was organized by Hamas, killed sixteen people and wounded 100.

Funding Terror Groups

Palestinian terrorist groups obtain the funds they need to conduct suicide bombings from many sources. In the past, the governments of some nearby Islamic countries, including Syria, Iraq, and Iran, gave huge sums of money to terror groups. For example, Iran, which is an Islamic state but not an Arab one, was at one time contributing $3 million a year to Hamas. Although some of that money paid for social services in the Occupied Territories, part of it funded terrorist activities.

Iraq was a major contributor to Palestinian terrorist groups until the Iraq War ousted dictator Saddam Hussein in 2003. In addition to donating money to the groups, Hussein also gave the families of suicide bombers rewards of as much as $25,000 in honor of the bombers who blew themselves up. Terror groups such as Hamas and Al-Aqsa Martyrs' Brigade also gave money to families of bombers, sometimes as monthly payments for the rest of their lives.

> **Hussein also gave the families of suicide bombers as much as $25,000**

Funds were also funneled to terrorist groups through allegedly charitable organizations such as Muslim Aid and the Islamic Relief Agency. These groups operated in the United States and other Western nations, where they collected money from sympathizers, mainly Arabs and Muslims. Israel believes that the Palestinian Authority funded al-Aqsa and Tanzim while Yasser Arafat headed the PA from 1993 to 2005. They claimed to have uncovered evidence of such payments in 2002, when Israeli soldiers raided PA offices while trying to fight suicide bombings and other terrorist attacks.

CHAPTER THREE

Background to the Arab-Israeli Conflict

When Ahmed Abu Khalil left his family's home in the West Bank village of Atil on the morning of July 12, 2005, he told his mother he was going to check on his grades from his high-school final exams. Instead, the eighteen-year-old student crossed into Israel on a suicide-bombing mission for the organization Islamic Jihad. He blew himself up outside the HaSharon mall in Netanya, killing five Israelis, including two sixteen-year-old girls. Lutfiah Abu Khalil had not known what her son was going to do, but she was not surprised. "For the past several years," she said, "he talked all the time about becoming a martyr." Lutfiah praised Ahmed as a "hero" and said she hoped fourteen-year-old Mahmoud would follow his older brother's example.

People around the world find it difficult to understand why someone like Ahmed would be willing to kill himself to hurt Israelis and how his mother could rejoice in his death. In the farewell video he recorded before the bombing, Ahmed said that Palestinians "have to retaliate for Israeli violations," referring to a truce that was then in operation in the conflict after the election of a new Palestinian leader. Palestinians' bitterness is intensified by the harsh conditions of their daily lives and the historical events that have shaped their world.

History of Palestine

Palestine is the historical name of a region on the eastern shore of the Mediterranean Sea that includes

▼ Members of Hamas march through a refugee camp in the Gaza Strip in April 2005.

parts of modern Israel and the Occupied Territories; in some definitions it also includes parts of Jordan. It has never been an independent state. For centuries, the region has been home to both Arabs and Jews; they have both governed the region at different times. Therefore, both Arabs and Jews claim Palestine as their traditional homeland.

The people who became known as Israelites, the forerunners of the Jews, first moved to the area that would become known as Palestine about 3,500 years ago. About five hundred years later, King David created the Kingdom of Israel there. For much of the next one thousand years, however, Israel was ruled by various conquerors, including the Romans, who in A.D. 63 named the area Judea. After Jews revolted twice against their rulers, the Romans drove them out of Judea in A.D. 135 and renamed the area Palaestina, which translates into English as Palestine.

Jewish Terrorism

At the time of Israel's birth, some Jews in Palestine also used terrorist tactics. In the 1940s, two Jewish groups waged campaigns against the Arabs and the British, who they saw as illegally occupying the region. Two Jewish terrorist groups, Irgun and the Stern Gang (named for the group's founder, Avraham Stern), both wanted to spread fear so that the British and Arabs would accept the creation of Israel on Jewish terms.

In 1944, the Stern Gang assassinated the British colonial secretary Lord Moyne in Cairo. In 1945, Irgun began bombing targets in Palestine, such as railroad sites and oil refineries. On July 22, 1946, Irgun terrorists blew up the King David Hotel in Jerusalem, which housed British government offices. Ninety-one British, Arab, and Jewish people died. In 1947, Irgun bombed buses, killing twenty-seven Arabs, Jews, and Britons. Its members threw grenades from a taxi into a cafe in Jerusalem, killing thirteen people.

In January 1948, Irgun exploded a truck bomb in the Arab city of Jaffa, killing twenty-six people. The Stern Gang, meanwhile, killed the Swedish UN mediator in Palestine, Count Folke Bernadotte in 1948.

The most infamous act of Jewish terrorism was the April 9, 1948, attack on the village of Deir Yasin. Irgun terrorists killed all two hundred fifty-four men, women, and children in the village. Many terrified Arabs began to flee the land marked for the creation of Israel.

After the creation of Israel, its prime minster, David Ben Gurion, got the terrorist groups to swear loyalty to the Israeli defense forces. Since 1948, there have been acts of Jewish terrorism, but they have been carried out by people acting alone. These acts include, for example, the 1994 massacre by an Jewish extremist of twenty-nine Palestinians in a mosque in Hebron.

◀ Rescuers search for survivors in the bombed King David Hotel, in Jerusalem, after it was blown up by Irgun in 1946.

During the seventh century, Muslim warriors originating from the Arabian Peninsula conquered most of the Middle East and spread Islam throughout the area. Many of the people of Palestine adopted Islam, along with Arabic culture and language. The region later fell under the control of various Islamic empires. Some, such as the Mamelukes of Egypt, were Arabs; others, like the Turkish Ottoman Empire that conquered the region in 1517, were not Arab. In 1918, when World War I ended, the defeated Ottoman Empire broke up. Great Britain began governing Palestine under a mandate, or license, from the League of Nations, a body created to encourage cooperation among nations.

A Jewish Homeland

During the nineteenth century, small groups of Jews had begun moving to Palestine from other countries. In 1896, a journalist in Austria, Theodor Herzl, wrote a pamphlet arguing that the Jews should create a homeland. He considered a number of locations, including the island of Cyprus and Uganda. Most European Jews argued that the homeland should be in Palestine. The movement to establish a Jewish state in Palestine is known as Zionism. (Zion is the name of a hill in Jerusalem.)

In 1917, the British foreign secretary James Balfour gave British backing to the creation of a Jewish state in Palestine. Many more Jews began to arrive in the region, with about 100,000 Jews settling there during the 1920s. Fearing that Jews could eventually win control of the area, Arabs began attacking them. The Jewish settlers set up an underground army, the Haganah, to defend themselves. They also established an unofficial government that looked after all aspects of Jewish society. Both Arabs and Jews inflicted terrorist attacks on the others.

> **The Jewish settlers set up an underground army, the Haganah, to defend themselves**

After World War II (1939–1945), many nations began supporting the creation of a Jewish nation as a refuge for survivors of the Holocaust, the Nazi German genocide which took the lives of six million Jews and three million other people. On November 29, 1947, the United Nations (UN), which had replaced the League of Nations, created a plan to partition (divide) Palestine almost equally into two nations—one for the 600,000 Jews and the other for the 1.2 million Arabs, all of whom lived in the region under British rule.

Israel—Born in Conflict

The Jews were willing to accept the plan and on May 14, 1948, Jewish leader David Ben Gurion declared the

A Statistical Portrait of 100 Suicide Bombers

On October 7, 2001, Ahmed abd al-Muneim Daraghmeh became the one-hundredth Palestinian suicide bomber since the first one in 1993. The 17-year-old member of Islamic Jihad killed Israeli Yair Mordechai when he detonated the bomb he was wearing near the entrance to Kibbutz Shluhot in the Beit She'an Valley. Of the first 100 suicide bombers, 66 belonged to Hamas and 34 to Islamic Jihad.

The bombers were all men and their average age was 21, with 67 bombers between the ages of 17 and 23. In the next few years, a handful of women and younger teenagers would also become bombers. Fifty-four of the first 100 bombers were from the Gaza Strip and 45 from the West Bank.

One bomber was an Arab who lived in Israel; at age 53, he was also the oldest. Eighty-six bombers were single and the rest married. Twenty-three bombers had an elementary school education, 31 were high school graduates, and 46 had attended college.

Seventy-five of the first 100 suicide bombers were killed while carrying out 67 separate missions; there are more deaths than individual attacks because several attacks involved multiple bombers. The other 25 bombers failed to carry out their terrorist operations because they were either intercepted by Israeli security forces or captured after their explosives failed to detonate.

independence of Israel. The Palestinian Arabs and neighboring Arab states, however, rejected the plan. Forces from Egypt, Jordan, Iraq, Syria, and Lebanon declared war on Israel and attacked it. The Israelis beat off the attacks, and on April 3, 1949, both sides agreed to a ceasefire. The Arab states refused to sign a peace treaty, which left both sides officially at war, although armistice agreements established a temporary frontier for Israel. During the war Israel had captured 50 percent more of Palestine than the UN had granted it in the 1947 partition plan. Of the remaining territory, the UN had set aside for a Palestinian state, Jordan was left in control of the West Bank, which it annexed in 1950. Egypt was left in control of the Gaza Strip.

The Palestinian Exodus

The Palestinians refer to the Israeli victory in the 1948 war as the Nakba, an Arabic word that means "disaster." In 1951, the United Nations welfare agency that looked after refugees estimated that about 860,000 Palestinian Arabs had left the region that was now under Israeli control. Most moved to refugee camps in Lebanon, Syria, and Jordan, and in the Gaza Strip and the West Bank. Many Palestinians claim that they were

▲ Palestinian refugees set up these temporary living quarters near Amman, in what is now Jordan, after fleeing the land on which they had previously lived in 1948, as tensions grew before the creation of Israel.

evicted from their homes by force. The real reasons so many people left are far more complex and controversial.

One likely reason for the exodus was the Arabs' fear of attack, first from Zionist terrorist groups and later from Israeli military forces. On April 9, 1948, members of the Jewish terrorist group Irgun massacred all 254 inhabitants of the Arab village of Deir Yasin. Some people believe the groups were engaged in a campaign to terrorize Arabs in order to consolidate and widen the territory that would be given to the new Jewish state.

The massacre at Dayr Yasin caused widespread panic among many Arabs.

They did not feel safe, and so they fled outside the proposed borders of Israel. Meanwhile Arab leaders proved weak at reassuring their people, particularly after the Arab–Israeli War began and went so badly for Arab forces. Some influential families fled, causing more panic; other Arabs voluntarily sold their land to Jews.

At the end of the war, the Arabs who fled had no homes to return to and became refugees. Palestinian anger is still strong because the refugees have not been allowed to return to the communities they claim as home.

The 1967 War

Israel also won wars against Arab armies in 1956, 1967, and 1973. The highly important 1967 war broke out when Syria and Egypt increased their military forces on Israel's frontiers, and Egypt tried to eject a United Nations peacekeeping force from Sinai, its border area with Israel. Israel launched strategic air and military strikes against Egypt, Syria, and Jordan before it could be attacked. The conflict is known as the Six-Day War, because it only took Israeli forces from June 5 to June 11 to defeat the Arab nations.

Victory in 1967 more than doubled the area controlled by Israel. It captured Gaza and Sinai from Egypt, the West Bank from Jordan, and the Golan Heights from Syria. Israel also took control of East Jerusalem, the part of the holy city whose western half it already controlled. About 600,000 Palestinians in the West Bank and tens of thousands more in Gaza came under Israeli control, while about 300,000 moved to neighboring states, most of them going to Jordan.

Negotiation, Not Terrorism

After the 1967 war, Palestinians increased their terror attacks against Israeli soldiers and civilians who occupied the Gaza Strip and West Bank. The Palestine Liberation Organization (PLO)—in Arabic, Munazzamat al-Tahrir Filastiniyyah—had been founded in 1964 as an umbrella organization composed of many smaller Palestinian groups. The PLO began coordinating and conducting terrorist attacks against Israeli targets.

Yasser Arafat (1929–2004) led the PLO from 1969 until his death and became the most revered Palestinian leader. Under his guidance as PLO chairman, the group became notorious worldwide for its daring, brutal attacks against Israelis in the Middle East and other parts of the world. The PLO's most infamous act of terrorism was the attack on Israeli athletes at the 1972 Summer Olympics in Munich, Germany by Black September, one of the many terrorist groups it directed.

In October 1973, another Arab-Israeli war began when Egypt and Syria launched coordinated attacks on Egypt's southwestern and nothern borders. Although the Arab armies fared better than in previous conflicts, they were again defeated. Arafat concluded that the Arab nations would never defeat Israel militarily. He began to believe that he needed to gain the political backing of other countries to help Palestinians force Israel to give up the contested territory so they could have their own nation. To do that, Arafat tried to change the PLO's image as a terrorist group to win international support.

A New Approach?

In a dramatic speech to the UN on November 13, 1974, Arafat claimed Palestinians were willing to give up their violent ways. Arafat's words had a

> **Yasser Arafat led the PLO from 1969 until his death and became the most revered Palestinian leader**

threatening tone, however: "Today I have come bearing an olive branch and a freedom fighter's gun. Do not let the olive branch fall from my hand."

Arafat's speech marked a historic turn in the conflict. It helped sway UN delegates to declare the Palestinians' right to have their own nation and won recognition of the PLO as the official representative for

▼ Palestinian terrorists in the Olympic Village in Munich, Germany, in 1972. In a high-profile siege, terrorists killed two members of the Israeli Olympic team and took nine more hostage. The hostages died during an attempt to free them as the terrorists prepared to take them on board an airplane.

Palestinians. Even though Israeli leaders hated Arafat because he was a terrorist, they had to begin dealing with him as the official Palestinian spokesman.

The Oslo Accords

Sporadic negotiations over the next two decades failed to achieve peace because the PLO continued to conduct terrorist activity against Israel, even though it often denied any involvement. In 1992, however, Israel and the PLO finally began meaningful talks in Oslo, Norway. The result was the Declaration of Principles (DOP), or Oslo Accords, which Arafat and Israel prime minister Yitzhak Rabin signed on September 13, 1993, in

Washington, D. C. Under the Accords, the PLO agreed to end terrorism and recognize Israel's right to exist. In return, Israel promised to withdraw from most areas of the West Bank and Gaza Strip and allow a degree of Palestinian self-government. It created an interim period of five years during which serious unresolved issues could be negotiated before the conclusion of a final peace deal. These issues included the right of Palestinian refugees to return to their homes and the end of Israeli settlement in the Occupied Territories.

An Illusion of Peace?

The Accords created the Palestinian Authority (PA) to exercise partial government of the West Bank and Gaza Strip. Voters elected Arafat president—the Arab term for the position is *rais*—and chose 88 legislators to serve on the Palestinian Legislative Council (PLC), which made laws that governed Palestinians in the Occupied Territories.

When Arafat and Rabin signed the Accords, U.S. president Bill Clinton persuaded them to shake hands for the press cameras, even though the two men despised each other. People around the world thought the gesture was symbolic of the end of the conflict and hoped peace would come to the Middle East.

On November 4, 1995, Amir shot Rabin to death in Tel Aviv because he claimed Rabin had betrayed Israel

In the next few years, the Israelis began withdrawing soldiers and civilians from the West Bank and Gaza. The plan was doomed, however, in large part because many Arabs and Israelis alike opposed it. Some Palestinians opposed it because they complained that Israel now claimed control of all of Jerusalem, a city that was holy to Muslims as well as Jews, and that soldiers and settlers were not leaving the West Bank and Gaza Strip fast enough. Some Israelis, meanwhile, were afraid that giving up any territory to the Palestinians threatened their country's future by creating another enemy nation on its borders. That fear was one factor that motivated Yigal Amir, a Jewish law student with extreme political views, to commit an act of violence against his own nation. On November 4, 1995, Amir shot and killed Rabin in Tel Aviv. Amir shot the Israeli prime minister because he claimed Rabin had betrayed Israel by agreeing to the Accords with the Palestinians.

The Accords Break Down

After Rabin's death, in the second half of the 1990s, new Israeli leaders who also feared the effects of the Accords began allowing more Jewish settlers into the Occupied Territories. Under the Accords, the creation of new settlements was to be suspended while

▲ A mourner prays at a shrine marking the place where Israeli prime minister Yitzhak Rabin was killed by an Israeli extremist.

their future was discussed. The new Israeli leaders claimed that building more Jewish settlements would make Israel safer by creating a buffer zone between Israel and its Arab enemies. But the influx of Jews angered Arabs, who believed the new settlements were a Jewish invasion of their land. This anger fueled more terrorism. In 1996, Hamas suicide bombers blew up several buses, killing sixty Israelis. In 1997, two simultaneous suicide bomb attacks in a Jerusalem market on July 30, 1997, killed 16 people and wounded 178.

In an attempt to end such violent acts, President Clinton persuaded Yasser Arafat and Israeli prime minister Ehud Barak to meet at Camp David, the U.S. presidential retreat, to settle their differences. Peace talks were held from July 11 to July 14, 2000, but they broke down after Arafat rejected Israel's proposal to withdraw all soldiers and most settlers from the Gaza Strip and West Bank. Although many observers believed the offer was a good basis for progress, Arafat claimed Israel had not made enough concessions on key issues. These issues included sharing control of Jerusalem, where Arabs dominated the eastern part of the city, and allowing Palestinians to return to their former homes in Israel. Arafat

Yasser Arafat: Hero or Terrorist?

Yasser Arafat always wore his kafiyeh, the traditional Arab head covering, draped over his right shoulder so that it resembled the outline of Palestine. It was a symbol of his desire for Palestinians to have their own nation. When Arafat died in a hospital in Paris, France, on November 11, 2004, he was a hero to many Palestinians. Most Israelis, however, considered Arafat a terrorist who had killed thousands through his leadership role in the Palestine Liberation Organization and as president of the Palestinian Authority.

In 1994, Arafat and two Israeli leaders—Yitzhak Rabin and Shimon Peres—won the 1994 Nobel Peace Prize for negotiating the 1993 Oslo Accords, an agreement that many hoped would end the Arab-Israeli conflict. In accepting the award, Arafat claimed, "Peace is in our interest: as only in an atmosphere of just peace shall the Palestinian people achieve their legitimate ambition for independence and sovereignty [self-rule]."

Despite his claim that day, Arafat failed to effectively clamp down on violence against Israelis and even praised Palestinians who committed terrorist attacks. After a suicide bombing in 2002 that killed 27 Israelis, Arafat praised the bomber with this remark: "We are all potential martyrs, the whole Palestinian people. Oh God, give me martyrdom like this." Such remarks contradicted his claims to reject terrorism. Most Western historians believe that Arafat's refusal to reject terrorism and effectively oppose it were the main obstacles to the creation of a Palestinian state under his leadership.

walked out of the peace talks, which then broke down.

The Second Intifada

Palestinians were angry the talks had failed because it meant another delay in getting their own nation. This anger bubbled over into violence on

September 28, 2000, when Israeli political leader Ariel Sharon visited the Temple Mount in East Jerusalem. The site is sacred to Judaism because it includes the remains of a Jewish temple the Romans destroyed in A.D. 70. However, Muslims also revere it as the spot where Muhammad ascended into Heaven in 610. Muslims call the site Al-Haram al-Sharif ("Noble Sanctuary") and it houses two historic mosques: Al-Aqsa and the golden

▼ Palestinians gathered on November 12, 2004, in the West Bank town of Ramallah for the funeral of Yasser Arafat.

The Right of Return

One of the most complex issues in the Arab-Israeli conflict is question of the right of Arabs to return to places in Israel where they once lived. About 800,000 Palestinians left Israel before or during the 1948 war. Arab leaders say that the Israelis should recognize a Palestinian "right to return." A 1948 United Nations resolution said that Palestinian "refugees wishing to return to their homes and live at peace with their neighbors should be permitted to do so at the earliest practical date."

Israel refuses to allow refugees in; it says that there is no room for them. It also argues that many Jews had to leave their homes in Palestine in 1948 in areas that came under Arab control. A return of the refugees would have profound consequences for Israel. Today, about 5.4 million of Israel's population of 6.6 million are Jews. The rest are mainly Israeli Arabs who stayed in Israel after the 1948 war. Counting descendants born since 1948, the number of Palestinian refugees has risen to more than four million. If they returned, Israeli Jews might become a minority in the country.

Israeli prime minister Ariel Sharon said in May 2005, "There will be no entry of Palestinian refugees into Israel." Palestinian Authority president Mahmoud Abbas maintains refugees should be able to return, but, in July 2005, he asked Arab countries sheltering refugees to grant them citizenship. Only Jordan did so. If refugees became citizens of other countries, they might lose their claim to homes they had not seen in decades.

Dome of the Rock, which is a Jerusalem landmark. Sharon's visit so enraged Arabs that they began rioting against Israeli citizens and soldiers. The violence marked the start of the second intifada, which is sometimes called the Al-Aqsa Intifada, after the mosque. The Al-Aqsa Martyrs' Brigade is also named after this holy place.

The second intifada began the Arab-Israeli conflict's most deadly era of suicide bombing. Thirty such attacks ocurred in the first year of the uprising alone. The first happened December 22, when three Israeli soldiers were injured at a roadside café in the Jordan Valley. Deadly attacks occurred on June 1, 2001, when twenty-one people were killed and 120 wounded outside a disco in Tel Aviv, and August 9, 2001, when fifteen people died and about 130 were injured at the Sbarro Pizzeria in Jerusalem.

Living With Despair

The second intifada made living conditions worse for many Palestinians in the Occupied Territories. To prevent terrorists from getting into Israel, the Israeli Defense Forces (IDF) frequently

▶ Children play in the Baqa'a refugee camp near Amman, Jordan. Conditions in the camp, the largest in Jordan, are overcrowded and cramped.

sealed the borders of the West Bank and Gaza, sometimes for days at a time. Palestinians could not travel to jobs in Israel, where between a third or a half of Palestinians work.

Even before the new security restrictions, the Palestinians suffered from low living standards, including a lack of educational opportunities, substandard housing, and military occupation by the IDF.

Most Palestinians live in cities like Ramallah, Bethlehem, Tulkarm, and Gaza City. Although some are affluent, the majority live in poverty due to unemployment that is often as high as 50 percent. The refugee camps in the Occupied Territories and in Jordan, Lebanon, and Syria are more crowded and less comfortable than the established cities.

The Palestinians' living conditions are made worse by weak and corrupt government. Under Yasser Arafat, for example, the Palestinian Authority channeled money that could have been used for social purposes to terrorist groups, and Palestinians widely believe that Arafat's old party, Fatah, is corrupt.

In 2005, the IDF withdrew from the Gaza Strip, having removed all Israeli settlements from the region. The Palestinian Authority, dominated by Fatah, took over government. Its power was challenged by Hamas, which has a reputation for good management of social programs among Palestinians. Hamas was successful in local elections, and its followers challenged PA security forces. Hamas finds willing listeners in the Occupied Territories and refugee camps who believe its claim that the plight of the Palestinians can only be improved by the destruction of Israel.

CHAPTER FOUR

Israel's Response to Palestinian Terrorism

Passover is one of Judaism's holiest periods. During Passover week in March 2002, suicide bombers struck six times, killing 49 people and wounding over 100 more. The deadliest blast occurred on March 27, when 30 people celebrating Passover died in a restaurant in Netanya. The suicide bombings were part of a wave of various types of terrorist attacks that month that took the lives of 140 Israelis. The huge death toll led Prime Minister Ariel Sharon on March 29 to announce the beginning of Operation Defensive Wall, Israel's toughest response ever to Palestinian terrorism.

Sharon proclaimed in a news conference that "The state of Israel is at war, a war against terror." He promised to do whatever was necessary to stop the attacks because "there is no compromise with terrorists." The planned anti-terrorism offensive would include Israeli military intervention in West Bank communities from which suicide bombers had come, mass arrests of terrorists, and assassination of terror group leaders.

The operation's first major effort was aimed at Yasser Arafat, the head of the Palestinian Authority (PA), who Sharon claimed was an "enemy (who) has established a coalition of terror against Israel."

Getting Tough On Terrorists

Even as Sharon was speaking, soldiers of the Israeli Defense Forces (IDF) were besieging the Mukata, an office complex in the West Bank city of Ramallah

that served as the PA headquarters. The IDF trapped Arafat inside the Mukata and kept him imprisoned there until October 2004, when he became seriously sick. At that time, the Israelis allowed Arafat to go to France to seek medical attention. The reason that Israel isolated Arafat in Ramallah was to weaken his control over Palestinians because he had continued to support terrorist activities despite his repeated promises to end them.

Arafat, however, was only one of many targets of the new Israeli offensive. IDF troops began rounding up terrorist leaders such as Marwan Barghouti, who headed the Al-Aqsa Martyrs' Brigade. In 2004, Barghouti was found innocent of charges involving the deaths of 31 people, but

▼ Palestinian boys stone a bulldozer and tanks as Israeli troops move in to impose a curfew in a village in the Gaza Strip in 2002.

he was convicted of five counts of murder in three bombing attacks and sentenced to five life-sentences in jail. The arrests of terrorist leaders like Barghouti were possible because IDF troops retook control of many West Bank communities that Palestinians had been governing since the Oslo Accords of 1993. After assuming control of those areas, IDF troops used tanks to patrol them and make it harder for terrorists to attack Israelis.

Deterring Terrorists

In order to weaken the groups launching the attacks, the IDF also began assassinating terrorist leaders in a policy they called "targeted killing." The best-known terrorist leader that Israel assassinated was Hamas founder Sheikh Ahmed Yassin. In March 2004, Yassin told a reporter he knew the Israelis wanted to kill him. Yassin added that he did not fear death because, "All my life I have dreamed of martyrdom." A week later, on March 23, the 67-year-old Yassin was killed by a missile fired from an IDF helicopter. The Israeli military used helicopters and planes to attack terrorists in Arab-controlled areas that were too dangerous for ground troops to enter.

Israel also tried to deter suicide attacks by punishing the families of bombers. The punishment was the destruction of their homes, usually by using a bulldozer to crush the house. They wanted to discourage other potential suicide bombers by showing them that their families would suffer for their actions. On January 29, 2003, Ali Jaara, a Palestinian policemen, killed 10 people when he blew himself up on a bus in Jerusalem. After IDF forces demolished his home, Yusuf Jaara, Ali's father, said, "I began my life in tents and now I've returned to living in tents." He added that he would have stopped his son if he had known his intentions.

Preventing Attacks

IDF patrols, assassinations, and home demolitions weakened terrorist groups. But the best way to protect Israelis was to keep suicide bombers from entering Israel and to make it hard for them to carry out an attack successfully if they did get in. The IDF tightened security on Israel's borders with the Gaza Strip and West Bank to try to keep bombers out. To enter Israel, people had to pass through security stations manned by soldiers, who checked for proper identification and searched people who seemed like possible threats. This group included people who acted suspicious, nervous, or fearful, and almost anyone carrying backpacks or bags that could contain bombs.

The IDF tried to keep bombers out by tightening security on Israel's borders with the Gaza Strip and West Bank

Being Afraid All The Time

People who are injured or killed are not the only victims of suicide bombings. The goal of terrorism is to make members of the targeted population, in this case Israelis, fearful of the next attack. In this sense, suicide bombers have been very successful. Nikki Hasson-Moss, who lives in Jerusalem, admits that she worries a lot about terrorist attacks. "My biggest fear," she said, "is of something happening to one of us (members of her family)."

She is especially afraid when riding the bus, a favorite target of suicide bombers. Hasson-Moss remembers how scared she became one day when a young man who looked Palestinian was carrying a backpack got on the bus she was riding. Hasson-Moss admitted, "I panicked" and began thinking, "He's going to blow himself up any second [and] now I'm going to die."

When nothing happened, she admitted that she "felt like an idiot." Yet her fear had been real and it was a terrible experience to go through. Millions of other Israelis have been terrorized by the same fears that filled Hasson-Moss that day. They worry about the future of their country, and they wonder if they will always be afraid.

An example of how the tightened security helped curb attacks occurred on June 25, 2005, when 21-year-old Wafa al-Biss was arrested while trying to enter Israel from the Gaza Strip. When al-Biss acted nervously, a search revealed that she had 20 pounds of explosives hidden beneath her clothes. A member of the Al-Aqsa Martyrs' Brigade, al-Biss later claimed that, "Since I was a little girl I wanted to carry out an attack."

Security Measures

Bombers who managed to get inside Israel had to deal with a variety of security measures that made it tougher for them to carry out their suicide missions. Israeli police were always watching for anyone who looked suspicious and often stopped people to question or search them. Buses were a favorite target of the bombers, so armed guards patrolled bus stops. Other targets, like nightclubs and restaurants, employed guards who inspected bags and other items carried by patrons before they would let them in. Businesses that might be targeted had metal detectors or bomb-sniffing dogs to find bombers. Some Israelis carried guns to defend themselves, particularly in Jewish communities in the West Bank and Gaza Strip. The security measures, like those put in place in U.S. airports after the September 11, 2001, suicide airplane attacks, were an inconvenience for many Israelis. They put up with them, however, because the measures made their lives safer.

A Security Fence

The peak year for Palestinian suicide bombings was 2002, at the start of the second intifada, when 35 attacks killed nearly 80 people. The wave of violence convinced Israel to began building a barrier along the West Bank, which was home to most of the bombers. Dr. Hanan Shai, a military strategist and reserve colonel in the Israel Defense Forces, explained why the barrier was necessary: "If you want to keep mosquitoes out, then you need a screen on the windows."

The barrier to keep out bombers and other terrorists is 400 miles (680 km) long. It consists of a concrete wall that, in some locations, is up to 25 feet (6 m) tall; barbed wire; and trenches that extend from either side of it. To get through the barrier, people have to pass through military checkpoints.

The barrier has been criticized for isolating Palestinians by making it difficult for them to travel into nearby Israeli cities to work, shop, or even receive medical attention. The barrier and other security measures that Israel began putting in place in 2002, however, combined to drastically reduce the number of attacks. IDF statistics indicated a 30 percent drop in the number of all types of terrorist attacks in 2003 compared to 2002. The

▼ Israeli troops check the identification documents of Palestinians entering the Old City of Jerusalem in 2002.

number of suicide bombings fell from a high of 35 in 2002 to twenty in 2003; 10 in 2004; and 3 in 2005 through October.

The reduction was due to an increase in the thwarting of attacks by stopping bombers by catching them at checkpoints or other places before they could complete their attacks. In 2004, the IDF thwarted 136 suicide bombers, and, in the first half of 2005, it stopped more than 90 bombers from entering Israel.

Movement Toward Peace

The only way to totally end suicide bombings, however, is to resolve the Arab-Israeli conflict. By 2005, there was new hope this might one day

happen. The 1993 Oslo Accords had laid the groundwork for Israel's withdrawal from the Gaza Strip and West Bank and the creation of a Palestinian state. In 2000, howeve, the two sides failed to reach agreement on final details of the plan, particularly relating to Israeli settlements in the Occupied Territories, the Palestinians' right to return, and the status of East Jerusalem. The second intifada began, keeping the two sides from making any further progress in negotiations.

In 2004, Israel decided on its own to withdraw completely from the Gaza

▼ Israeli prime minister Ariel Sharon (left) meets new Palestinian leader Mahmoud Abbas at talks in Egypt in February 2005.

The Barrier Conflict

The controversy over the West Bank barrier is summed up by the names the two sides have given the imposing 400 mile physical barrier composed of fences, walls, and trenches. Israelis call it a "separation fence," "security fence," or "anti-terrorist fence." Palestinians have named it the "Jidar Al-Fasl Al-Unsuri," Arabic for "racial segregation wall," and also use the English term "apartheid wall." However, Israelis and their supporters argue that the wall cannot have a racial aim, because TK million Israeli Arabs live inside the wall.

Israelis claim they need the wall to keep suicide bombers and other terrorists from entering their country and killing people. The Palestinians believe the wall is intended to consolidate Israeli control over land some Palestinians still claim. A secondary complaint is that Israel designed the barrier's route so that it would extend into territory occupied by Palestinians, sometimes by several miles. Palestinians are also angry that the barrier has made their life harder by making it difficult to travel to Israeli cities where they work, shop, and go for medical care. Palestinians and human rights groups claim that about 200,000 Palestinians will be adversely affected by it.

After a group of Palestinian villages affected by the wall filed a joint lawsuit, the Supreme Court of Israel in 2004 ruled that part of the barrier near Jerusalem violated the rights of Palestinians. The World Court backed the decision. The Israeli court ordered more than 20 miles of the wall to be re-routed, which was done shortly afterward.

▼ The Israeli government believes that the security barrier will protect Israel from terrorists entering from the West Bank.

Palestinian Victims

On July 23, 2003, an Israeli F-16 war plane bombed an apartment in Gaza City to kill Salah Shehadeh, a Hamas terrorist leader. But the bomb also killed 13 innocent bystanders, including his wife, his daughter, and eight other children.

Since the second intifada began on September 28, 2000, more than 3,500 Palestinians have died in Israeli military operations designed to protect Israel from terrorists. Palestinians, including young children, have been wounded or killed in riots, gun battles between soldiers and militants, and Israeli attacks on terrorist strongholds. Terrorist groups use the anger some Palestinians feel about such accidental deaths to recruit suicide bombers.

Strip and partially from the West Bank. Under the disengagement plan, Israel planned to remove about 9,100 Israelis from twenty-one settlements in the Gaza Strip and four in the northern West Bank, and abandon numerous IDF facilities. The plan, however, would leave about 200,000 Israelis in other West Bank settlements. Although many Israelis opposed the withdrawal because it seemed to be a concession to Palestinians, Sharon claimed it would strengthen Israel by making its remaining territory easier to defend.

A New Leader

Some Palestinians, including PA chairman Yasser Arafat, also opposed the plan because of the continued Israeli presence in the West Bank. After Arafat died on November 11, 2004, however, Mahmoud Abbas was elected the head of the Palestinian Authority. Abbas backed the Israeli withdrawal plan. He thought it was a significant step toward ending the violence that has hurt both Arabs and Israelis.

Sharon and Abbas met at Sharm el-Sheikh, Egypt, on February 8, 2005 to agree to a truce. In the next months, the truce was broken by three suicide bombings: in Tel Aviv in February; in Netanya in July; and in Hadera in October. Each bombing killed five people. The bombers were from Islamic Jihad, which opposed the withdrawal plan. Hamas, on the other hand, had suspended its terrorist operations while it waited to see if diplomacy might succeed. Abbas condemned the attacks because they jeopardized a chance to make progress in ending the conflict. He said of the second attack, "It's a crime against the Palestinian people."

Israel withdrew from the Gaza Strip in August 2005. Although difficult issues were left to resolve, many Israelis hoped that the withdrawal would be a step toward ending the Arab-Israeli conflict and the Palestinian suicide bombings that are part of it.

Time Line

1948	April 9: Jewish terrorists massacre villagers at Deir Yasin. May 14: Israel declares independence. May 15: Arab states attack Israel in the first Arab–Israeli War.
1949	April 3: A ceasefire ends the Arab–Israeli War.
1967	June 5–June 11: Six-Day War. Israel's victory leaves it in control of the West Bank and Gaza Strip.
1972	Palestinian terrorists attack Israeli athletes at the Munich Olympics.
1983	October 23: First suicide bomber attacks U.S. Marines in Beirut, Lebanon.
1987	Palestinians launch the first intifada.
1993	April 16: First suicide bomb attack in the Israeli-Palestinian conflict. September 13: Israel and the Palestinians sign the Oslo Accords.
1994	Yasser Arafat, Yitzhak Rabin, and Shimon Peres win the Nobel Peace Prize.
1995	November 4: An Israeli extremist assassinates Prime Minister Yitzhak Rabin.
2000	July 14: Yasser Arafat walks out of peace talks in the United States. September 28: Ariel Sharon's visit to Temple Mount sparks protests that lead to the second intifada.
2001	March: Ariel Sharon becomes prime minister of Israel.
2002	Suicide bombings in Israel reach a peak of thirty-five within one year.
2004	March 29: Israeli forces kill Sheikh Ahmed Yassin, founder of Hamas. November 11: Death of Yasser Arafat.
2005	February 8: Ariel Sharon holds peace talks with PA leader Mahmoud Abbas. August: Israel withdraws from all settlements in the Gaza Strip. September: Israeli Supreme Court orders government to review the route of the security barrier between Israel and the West Bank.

Glossary

buffer zone: an empty or neutral area between two hostile forces.

checkpoint: a place on a road or other route where travelers' identities are checked.

extremist: someone who holds radical beliefs and rejects any form of compromise.

Holocaust: the Nazi campaign of mass murder of millions of Jews and other people in Germany before and during World War II (1939–1945).

jihad: in Islam, a battle waged as a religious duty; used both for a personal battle against doubt and for battles against perceived enemies of Islam.

intifada: Arabic for "shaking off"; a name given to two periods of violent Palestinian unrest against Israelis, from 1987 to 1993 and from 2000 to 2004.

Islamist: a Muslim who believes that Islam should be the basis of all forms of government and culture.

mandate: an order given by the League of Nations for one of its member countries to establish a government over another area.

massacre: the cruel killing of many, usually defenseless, victims.

mosque: a building used by Muslims for worship.

nationalist: a person who believes in the importance of his or her nation and its culture and interests.

occupation: the control of an area of land by a foreign government.

Passover: a Jewish religious holiday celebrating the Hebrews' escape from slavery in Egypt.

partition: the legal division of a land into two or more nations.

self-government: a government controlled by the inhabitants of an area rather than by an outside force.

truce: a halt in hostilities agreed upon by the opposing sides.

refugee: a person who has been forced to flee from his or her home by danger, such as warfare or disaster.

Zionism: the movement advocating the creation of a Jewish homeland in the region of Palestine.

Further Reading

Books

Alger, Neil (ed.) *The Palestinians and the Disputed Territories* (World's Hot Spots). Greenhaven Press, 2003.

Brexel, Bernadette, and Holly Cefery. *Yasser Arafat* (Middle East Leaders). Rosen Publishing Group, 2003.

Broyles, Matthew. *The Six-Day War* (War and Conflict in the Middle East). Rosen Publishing Group, 2004.

Gallagher, Michael. *Israel And Palestine* (Flashpoints). Smart Apple Media, 2005.

Gunderson, Cory Gideon. *The Israeli-Palestinian Conflict* (World in Conflict: the Middle East). Abdo and Daughters Publishing, 2003.

Hayhurst, Chris. *Israel's War of Independence* (War and Conflict in the Middle East). Rosen Publishing Group, 2003.

King, John. *Israel and Palestine* (Middle East). Raintree 2005.

Miller, Debra A. (ed.) *Arab-Israeli Conflict* (Lucent Library of Conflict in the Middle East). Lucent Books, 2004.

Rosaler, Maxine. *Hamas: Palestinian Terrorists* (Inside the World's Most Infamous Terrorist Organizations). Rosen Publishing Group, 2002.

Wingate, Katherine. *The Intifadas* (War and Conflict in the Middle East). Rosen Publishing Group, 2003.

Web Sites

BBC News In-Depth: Israel and the Palestinians
news.bbc.co.uk/1/hi/in_depth/middle_east/2001/israel_and_the_palestinians/default.stm

CNN.com Mideast: Land of Conflict
edition.cnn.com/SPECIALS/2003/mideast/

NPR: The Mideast: A Century of Conflict
www.npr.org/news/specials/mideast/history/

BBC News Profile: Ariel Sharon
news.bbc.co.uk/1/hi/world/middle_east/1154622.stm

BBC News: Israel's History of Bomb Blasts from 2000 to 2005
news.bbc.co.uk/1/hi/world/middle_east/1197051.stm

Index